ROUSSEAU

LOVER OF HIMSELF,
A COMEDY

Daniel Boden

Simon Critchley

JEAN-JACQUES

NARCISSUS, OR THE

A

Translated by

Afterword by

JEAN-JACQUES ROUSSEAU

—

NARCISSUS,
OR
THE LOVER
OF HIMSELF,
A COMEDY

—

Translated by DANIEL BODEN

Afterword by SIMON CRITCHLEY

Contra Mundum Press   New York · London · Melbourne

Translation of *Narcisse, ou l'Amant de lui-même* © 2015 Daniel Boden. Afterword © 2015 Simon Critchley. Preface & play text translated from Jean-Jacques Rousseau, *Collection complète des œuvres*, Vol. 8 (Geneva: Du Peyrou and Moultou, 1782). This text was made available on www.rousseauonline.ch, with editorial & digitization credits given to Professor Joseph Milton Gallanar.

First Contra Mundum Press Edition 2015.

Library of Congress Cataloguing-in-Publication Data

Rousseau, Jean-Jacques, 1712–1778
[Narcisse. English.]

Narcissus, or The Lover of Himself, a Comedy / Jean-Jacques Rousseau; translated from the original French by Daniel Boden

—1ˢᵗ Contra Mundum Press Edition
128 pp., 5×8 in.

ISBN 9781940625133

   I. Rousseau, Jean-Jacques
  II. Title.
 III. Boden, Daniel.
  IV. Translator.
   V. Critchley, Simon.
  VI. Afterword.

2015951427

For performance rights, contact info@contramundum.net

For Michæl Henry Heim,
thank you for teaching me
your principles of translation

CONTENTS

PREFACE

I wrote this comedy at the age of eighteen, & I kept myself from showing it for as long as I held onto some regard for my reputation as an Author. I finally had enough courage to publish it, but I will never have enough to say anything about it. Here then, the matter is not of my play, but of myself.

I must, despite my reluctance, speak of myself; I must either recognize the wrongs attributed to me, or justify myself concerning them. I truly feel that the weapons will not be evenly matched; for I will be attacked with mockery, and I will defend myself only with reason: But provided that I convince my adversaries, I worry very little about persuading them; while working to deserve my own esteem, I have learned to make do without that of others, who, for the most part, make do without my own. But if it hardly matters to me whether people think well or ill of me, it does matter to me that no one be correct in thinking ill of me; and it matters to the truth that I upheld that its defender be not accused of precisely having lent it his help only out of caprice or vanity, without loving and without knowing it.

The side that I took in the question[i] I examined some years ago did not fail to create for me a multitude of adversaries[1] perhaps more attentive to the interests of lettered men than to the honor of literature. I had foreseen this & very well suspected that their behavior in this instance would prove to be in my favor more than all of my discourses. Indeed, they disguised neither their surprise, nor their chagrin at the fact that an Academy showed its integrity so inopportunely. They spared it neither indiscreet invective, nor even untruths,[2] which attempt to weaken the weight of its judgment. Nor was I forgotten in their declamations. Many tried to refute me openly: The wise were able to see with what force, and the public with what success they did this. The cleverer ones, knowing the danger of directly combatting demonstrated truths, handily diverted onto my person an attention that should have been given only to my reasoning, and the examination of the accusations that they brought against me has erased the memory of the more serious accusations that I myself brought against them. To these it is therefore necessary to respond once and for all.

They claim that I do not believe one word of the truths that I have upheld, and that in demonstrating a proposition, I did not fail to believe its opposite. That is to say, I proved such extravagant things that it can be affirmed that I could only maintain them as a game. What a great honor they render to the science that serves as the foundation to all the others; and we must believe that the art of reasoning is largely in the service of the discovery of truth when we see it used successfully to demonstrate follies!

They claim that I do not believe one word of the truths that I have upheld; this is undoubtedly a new and convenient way on their part to answer these arguments without response, to refute even Euclid's proofs, and all that has been demonstrated in the universe. It seems to me that those who so rashly accuse me of speaking against my thoughts do not themselves have any great scruples at speaking against their own: For they have assuredly found nothing in my writings or in my behavior that should have inspired in them this idea, as I will shortly prove; and it is not permissible for them to ignore the fact that once a man speaks seriously, we must think that he believes what he says, unless his actions or his discourses belie it, and even that does not always suffice to guarantee that he believes nothing of it.

They can therefore shout as much as they like, that in declaring myself against the pursuit of knowledge I spoke against my feelings; to such a rash assertion, equally devoid of both proof & likelihood, I give but one reply; it is short and energetic, and I politely ask them to consider it as it is delivered.

IV

They further claim that my behavior is contradictory to my principles, and it must not be doubted that they do employ the second charge to establish the first; for there are many people that know how to find proofs for that which is not. They will say then that in making music and writing verse, it is graceless to lower the fine arts, and that in the literature that I pretend to despise, there are a thousand occupations more praiseworthy than writing Comedies. It is also necessary to respond to this accusation.

Firstly, even if this were admitted in all its rigor, I say that it would prove that I behave badly, but not that I do not speak in good faith. If it were permitted to draw from men's actions the proof of their feelings, it would be necessary to say that love of justice is banished from all hearts and that there is not a single Christian on the earth. Show me men whose actions are always a consequence of their maxims and I will pass condemnation upon mine. Such is the lot of humanity: Reason shows us the goal and the passions lead us away from it. And were it true that I do not act according to my principles, that alone would not make it right to accuse me of speaking against my feelings, nor to accuse my principles of falseness.

But if I wanted to pass condemnation on this point, it would suffice for me to compare the times to reconcile things. I have not always had the good fortune to think as I act. Longtime seduced by the prejudices of my century, I took study to be the only occupation worthy of a wise man, I beheld the pursuit of knowledge only with respect, and the learned only with admiration.[3] I did not understand that one could go astray in always demonstrating wisdom, or do wrong in always speaking of it. It is only after having seen things close up that I learned to esteem them at their worth; and even though in my research, I always found *satis loquentiæ, sapientiæ parum*,[ii] I needed much reflection, much observation, and much time to destroy the illusion I had of all this vain scientific pomp. It is not astonishing that during those times of prejudice and error, in which I so highly esteemed the status of Author, I sometimes aspired to achieve it myself. And hence were composed the Verses and most of the other Writings which came from my plume, & among others, this little Comedy. It would perhaps be harsh to reproach me today for these amusements of my youth, and it would at least be wrong to accuse me of having thereby contradicted the principles that were not yet mine. It has been quite some time since I made any type of claim to these things; and to hazard giving them to the public in these circumstances after having had the prudence to hold on to them for such a long time is to say that I disdain equally the praise and the blame that may be due to them, for I no longer think as the Author whose work they are. They are illegitimate children whom one still caresses with pleasure while blushing at being their father, to whom one bids his last farewells, & whom one sends out to seek their fortunes, without caring much of what they will become.

But this is to reason too much according to chimerical suppositions. If I am unreasonably accused of cultivating the Letters that I scorn, I defend myself unnecessarily; for if the charge were true, there would not be any inconsistency therein: This is what is left for me to prove.

For that, I will follow, as is my custom, the easy and simple method that suits the truth. I will re-establish the state of the question, I will newly expound upon my sentiment; and I expect that upon this exposé I will be shown how my actions betray my discourses. As for my adversaries, they will not keep themselves from responding, they who possess the marvelous art of arguing for and against all sorts of subjects. They will begin, as is their custom, by establishing another question according to their fancy; they will make me resolve it as it suits them: To attack me more conveniently, they will make me reason, not in my manner, but in theirs: They will skillfully turn aside the eyes of the reader from the essential object to set them to the right and to the left; they will fight a ghost & will claim to have vanquished me: But I will have done what I have to do, & thus I begin.

"The pursuit of knowledge is good for nothing & does nothing but harm, for it is bad by its nature. It is no more separable from vice than ignorance is from virtue. All lettered peoples have always been corrupt; all ignorant peoples have been virtuous: In a word, there are no vices except among the learned, neither are there virtuous men apart from he who knows nothing. Therefore, there is a way for us to become honest people again: It is to hurry ourselves in proscribing the pursuit of knowledge and learned men, to burn our libraries, to close our Academies, our Colleges, our Universities, and to plunge back into all the barbarism of the first centuries."

That is what my adversaries have very finely refuted: But never have I said, nor thought a single word of all that, & nothing could be imagined that would be more opposed to my system than this absurd doctrine that they have the goodness to attribute to me. But here is what I have said and what no one has refuted at all.

The question at hand was whether the restoration of the sciences & the arts contributed to the purification of our morals.

In demonstrating, as I did, that our morals were not at all purified,[4] the question was more or less resolved.

But it implicitly contained another more general and more important question on the influence that the cultivation of knowledge muſt have on people's morals on all occasions. It is this queſtion, of which the firſt is a mere consequence, that I proposed to examine with care.

I began with the facts, and I showed that morals have degenerated among all the people of the world, to the extent that the taſte for ſtudy & Letters has ſpread among them.

This was not enough; for without being able to deny that these things always worked together, it could be denied that one brought about the other: I therefore applied myself to showing this necessary link. I made it seen that the source of our errors on this point comes from the fact that we confuse our vain and treacherous knowledge with the sovereign Intelligence that sees at a glance the truth of all things. The pursuit of knowledge, taken in an abſtract manner, deserves all of our admiration. Man's mad pursuit of knowledge is worthy only of mockery and scorn.

The taſte for Letters among a people always announces the beginning of corruption, which it very promptly accelerates. For this taſte can only be born in an entire nation of two bad sources which ſtudy maintains and enlarges in turn; ſpecifically, laziness and the desire to diſtinguish oneself. In a well-conſtituted State, each citizen has his duties to fulfill & these important cares are too dear to him to leave him the leisure of attending to frivolous ſpeculations.

In a well-constituted State, all citizens are so equal that none can be preferred to others as the most learned or even as the most skilled, but at most as the best: Even this distinction is often dangerous, for it makes for liars and hypocrites.

The taste for Letters, which is born of the desire to distinguish oneself, necessarily produces ills infinitely more dangerous than all of the good it does is useful; in the end it makes those who succumb to it very unscrupulous about the means of success. The first Philosophers made a great reputation for themselves by teaching men the practice of their duties and the principles of virtue. But soon these precepts having become common, it was necessary to distinguish oneself in following contrary routes. Such is the origin of the absurd systems of the Leucippuses, Diogeneses, Pyrrhos, Protagorases, Lucretiuses. The Hobbeses, Mandevilles, and a thousand others have tried to distinguish themselves even among us; and their dangerous doctrines have borne such fruit that, although we may still have some true Philosophers, ardent to remind our hearts of the laws of humanity and virtue, it is horrifying to see to what point our century of reason has pushed the contempt of man and citizen into its maxims.

The taste for letters, philosophy, and the fine arts, annihilates the love of our first duties and of true glory. Once talents have invaded the honors due to virtue, everyone wants to be an agreeable man and no one worries about being a good man. From this is born this other inconsistency, that we reward men only for those qualities that do not depend on them: For our talents are born with us, only our virtues belong to us.

The first and almost only cares that we give to our education are the fruits & seeds of these ridiculous prejudices. It is in order to teach us Letters that we are tormented in our miserable youth: We know all the rules of grammar before having heard of the duties of man; we know all that has happened up until the present before we have been told a single word of what we are to do; and provided that we practice our babble, no one worries whether we know how to act or think. In a word, it is only prescribed to be learned in the things that are of no use to us at all; and our children are brought up precisely as the ancient athletes of the public games, who, ultimately dedicating their robust limbs to a useless and superfluous exercise, kept themselves from ever using them in any profitable work.

The taste for Letters, philosophy, and the fine arts softens bodies and souls. Working at a desk makes men delicate, weakens their temperament, and the soul keeps its vigor with difficulty when the body has lost its own. Study wears down the machine, drains spirits, destroys strength, enervates courage, & that alone is enough to show that it is not for us: This is how we become cowardly and pusillanimous, incapable of resisting both pain and passions. Everyone knows how much inhabitants of cities are unfit to support the labors of war and the reputation of lettered men in tales of bravery is not unknown.[5] Now nothing is more justly suspect than the honor of a coward.

So many reflections upon the weakness of our nature often serve only to turn us away from generous endeavors. Because we meditate upon the miseries of humanity, our imagination overwhelms us with their weight and too much foresight deprives us of our courage by depriving us of our security. It is in vain that we claim to arm ourselves against unforeseen accidents: "What if knowledge, trying to arm us with new defenses against natural mishaps, has imprinted in our fancy their magnitude and weight, more than her reasons and subtleties to protect us from them?"[iii]

The taste for philosophy slackens all bonds of esteem and goodwill, which tie men to society, and this is perhaps the most dangerous of all the evils that it engenders. The charm of study soon renders all other attachment insipid. Moreover, by thinking about humanity, by observing men, the Philosopher learns to appreciate them according to their worth, and it is difficult to really have affection for that which one despises. Soon he reunites in his person all the interest that virtuous men share with their peers: His contempt for others turns to the profit of his pride; his self-love increases in the same proportion as his indifference to the rest of the universe. The family, the fatherland, become for him empty words without meaning: He is neither parent, nor citizen, nor man; he is a Philosopher.

At the same time that the cultivation of knowledge in some way draws from the press the Philosopher's heart, in another sense, it commits to it that of the man of Letters and always with an equal prejudice for virtue. Every man that keeps himself busy with agreeable talents wants to please, to be admired, and he wants to be admired more than another. Public applause belongs to him alone: I would say that he does everything to obtain it, if he did not do even more to deprive his competitors of it. From this are born on one side the refinements of taste and politeness; vile and base flattery, seductive, insidious, puerile cares, which, in the long run, shrink the soul and corrupt the heart; and on the other side, jealousies, rivalries, hatreds of famed Artists, perfidious calumny, treachery, betrayal, and all that is most cowardly, and heinous in vice. If the Philosopher despises men, the Artist soon makes himself despised by them, and in the end both cooperate to make them despicable.

There is more; and of all the truths that I proposed for the consideration of wise men, this is the most astonishing and the most cruel. Our writers all regard as the masterpiece of the politics of our century the pursuit of knowledge, the arts, luxury, trade, laws, & other bonds, which tighten among men the knots of society[6] by personal interest and thereby place them all in mutual dependence, give them reciprocal needs and common interests, and oblige each of them to cooperate for the happiness of others in order to be able to make their own. These ideas are undoubtedly beautiful and are presented in a favorable light: But upon examining them attentively and impartially, the advantages that they initially seem to present are found to have much that can be cut down to size.

It is therefore quite a marvelous thing to have placed men in the impossibility of living among themselves without bearing prejudice against, supplanting, deceiving, betraying, and destroying each other! We must henceforth keep ourselves from ever being seen as we really are: For, for every two men whose interests align, there are perhaps a hundred thousand opposed to them, and there is no other means to succeed but to deceive or ruin all those people. This is the deathly source of violence, betrayal, perfidy, and all the horrors that are necessarily demanded by a state of things where each, pretending to work for the fortune or reputation of others, only seeks to raise his above them and at their expense.

What have we gained in this? Lots of babble, wealthy men and sophists, that is to say, enemies of virtue and common sense. On the other hand, we have lost innocence and morals. The masses crawl in misery; all are slaves of vice. Uncommitted crimes are already in the bottom of hearts, and the only thing staying their execution is that the assurance of impunity is lacking.

What a strange and deathly constitution where accumulated riches always facilitate the means to accumulate even greater ones and where it is impossible for he who has nothing to acquire something; where the good man has no means to escape misery; where the most knavish are the most honored; and where one must necessarily renounce virtue to become an honorable man! I know that the declaimers have said this all a hundred times; but they said it in declamations, and I say it upon reason; they have perceived the evil, and I discover its causes, & above all, I make one very consoling and useful thing apparent in showing that all these vices do not so much belong to man, but to man poorly governed.[7]

Such are the truths that I have developed and tried to prove in the diverse writings that I have published on this matter. Here now are the conclusions that I have drawn from them.

Knowledge is not at all made for man in general. He strays incessantly in search of it; and if he sometimes obtains it, it is almost always to his detriment. He is born to act and think, and not to reflect. Reflection only serves to make him unhappy without making him better or wiser: It makes him regret good things past and impedes him from enjoying the present: It shows him a happy future in order to seduce him by imagination and to torment him by desires and the unhappy future to make him feel it in advance. Study corrupts his morals, alters his health, destroys his temperament, and often spoils his reason; if it taught him something, I would still find him rather poorly compensated.

I admit that there are some sublime geniuses who know how to penetrate the veils in which truth is enveloped, a few privileged souls, capable of resisting the foolishness of vanity, base jealousy, and other passions that engender the taste for Letters. The small number of those who have the good fortune to possess all of these qualities are the light & honor of humankind; it is for them alone that it is appropriate to exercise themselves in study for the benefit of all, and this very exception confirms the rule; for if all men were like Socrates, then knowledge would not be harmful to them, but they would have no need of it.

Every people which has morals, and which consequently reſpects its laws and does not want to refine its ancient cuſtoms at all, muſt carefully protect itself from the pursuit of knowledge, and above all from the learned, whose sententious and dogmatic maxims would soon teach it to scorn its cuſtoms and laws, which a nation can never do without corrupting itself. The slighteſt change in cuſtoms, even if it were advantageous in some regard, always turns to the detriment of morals. For cuſtoms are the morality of the people; and as soon as it ceases to reſpect them, its only guide is its passions and its only reſtraint is the law, which can sometimes contain the wicked, but never make them good. Furthermore, once the philosopher has taught the people to scorn its cuſtoms, it soon finds the secret to eluding its laws. Thus I say that a people's morals are like a man's honor; it is a treasure that muſt be preserved, but that cannot be recovered once it has been loſt.[8]

But once a people is corrupted to a certain point, whether the pursuit of knowledge contributed to this or not, is it necessary to banish it or preserve the people from it in order to make it better or to prevent it from becoming worse? This is another queſtion in which I positively declared myself for the negative. For firſtly, since a vicious people never comes back to virtue, this is not about making good those who no longer are so, but to conserve as such those who already have the good fortune of being good. In the second place, the same causes that corrupted the people sometimes serve to prevent an even greater corruption; it is in this way that he who has spoiled his temperament by an indiscreet use of medicine is forced to have recourse to doctors to keep himself alive; it is in this way that the arts & the pursuit of knowledge, after having hatched the vices, are necessary to prevent them from turning into crimes; they cover them at least with a varnish that does not allow the poison to spread so freely. They destroy virtue, but leave its public simulacrum,[9] which is always a beautiful thing. They introduce in its place politeness and proprieties, and for the fear of appearing wicked, they substitute that of appearing ridiculous.

Thus I suggest, and I have already said this more than once, that we allow the existence and even the careful maintenance of the Academies, Colleges, Universities, Libraries, Spectacles, and all other amusements that can make some sort of diversion for the wickedness of men, and prevent them from occupying their idleness with more dangerous things. For in a country where it would no longer be a question of honest people & good morals, it would still be better to live with rascals than with brigands.

I now ask where is the contradiction in cultivating myself the tastes whose progress I approve? This is no longer about bringing the people to do good,

for it is sufficient to simply distract them from doing evil; they must be busied with inanities to turn
them away from bad actions; they must be amused
instead of preached to. If my Writings have edified
the small number of good people, I did them all the
good that depended on me, and maybe I am still of
service to them if I offer objects of distraction to the
others, which prevent them from thinking of them.
I would esteem myself only too fortunate to have a
hiss-worthy Play to put on everyday if, at this price
I could keep at bay the evil designs of even just one
of my Spectators for two hours and save the honor
of the daughter or wife of his friend, the secret of
his confidant, or the fortune of his creditor. When
there are no longer any morals, it is necessary only
to think of public order and it is known well enough
that Music and Spectacles are some of its most important objects.

If there remains some difficulty in my justification, I dare say it boldly; it is neither with regards
to the public, nor to my adversaries; it is with regard
to myself alone: For it is only in observing myself
that I can judge whether I must count myself among
that small number, and whether my soul is in a state
to bear the burden of literary exercises. I have felt
more than once their danger; more than once have
I abandoned them with the plan of taking them up
no more and, renouncing their seductive charm, I

have sacrificed at the cost of my heart's peace the only pleasures that could still soothe it. If in the languors that overwhelm me, if at the end of a difficult and painful career, I have dared to take them up again for a few moments to soothe my pains, at the very least I believe that I have put into it neither enough interest nor enough pretension to deserve the just reproaches that I have made to Lettered men for the same reason.

I needed a trial to attain an understanding of myself, and I went through it without hesitation. After having recognized the condition of my soul as a literary success, I needed to examine it as a literary failure. I now know what to think of it and I can subject the public to the worst of it. My play had the fate it deserved and that I had foreseen; but, despite the near annoyance that it caused me, I left the performance much happier with myself, and more rightfully so than if it had been a success.

Thus I advise those who are so intent on seeking to reproach me to be so good as to study my principles better and to observe my behavior better, before accusing me of contradiction and inconsistency. If they ever perceive that I am beginning to seek public approval, or that I grow vain from having written pretty songs, or that I blush for having written bad Comedies, or that I seek to injure the reputation of my competitors, or that I affect to speak evil of the great men of my century in an effort to lift me up to their level by lowering them to mine, or that I aspire to a position in an Academy, or that I pay court to women of influence, or that I laud the idiocies of the great, or that, no longer wanting to live from the work of my hands, I hold in ignominy the trade that I chose for myself and take steps to amass riches; if they remark, in a word, that the love of reputation makes me forget that of virtue, I beg them to bring it to my attention, even publicly, and I promise to throw my writings and my Books immediately into the fire, and to admit to all the errors with which they will be pleased to reproach me.

While waiting, I will write Books, I will make Verses and Music, if I have the talent, time, strength, and will to do so; I will continue to say quite frankly all the evil that I think of Letters and of those who cultivate them,[10] and I will believe that I am worth no less for it. It is true that it will be possible to say someday: This professed enemy of the sciences and the arts still wrote and published Plays; and this imputation will be, I admit, a very bitter satire, not upon me, but upon my century.

ENDNOTES

1. I am assured that many find it bad that I call my adversaries
my adversaries, and that seems to me rather believable in a century where one no longer dares to call anything by its name. I
have also learned that each of my adversaries complains, when
I answer other objections than his own, that I am wasting time
fighting against chimeras; which proves to me something that I
already suspected, namely that they do not waste a single moment of their own time listening to one another. As for me, it
is a pain that I believed I was obligated to take, and I read nu-
merous writings that they have published against me, from the
first response with which I was honored up to the four German
sermons among which one starts more or less in this manner:
*My brothers, if Socrates came back among us & observed the flour-
ishing state of knowledge in Europe; what am I saying, in Europe?
In Germany; what am I saying, in Germany? In Saxony; what am
I saying, in Saxony? In Leipzig; what am I saying, in Leipzig? In
this university. Thus seized with astonishment and penetrated with
respect, Socrates would sit down modestly among our schoolboys;
and with us, receiving our lessons with humility, he would soon lose
the ignorance of which he so justly complained.* I read all of that
and only made a few responses to it. Maybe I once again made
too many, but I am quite at ease knowing that these gentle-
men found them agreeable enough to be jealous of the preference. For the people who are shocked by the word *adversaries*,

I wholeheartedly consent to abandon it with them, provided that they be so kind as to indicate to me another by which I may designate, not only all those who have fought against my sentiment, whether in writing, or more carefully and more at ease in the circles of women and great minds, where they were quite certain that I would not go to defend myself, but also those who, now pretending to believe that I have no adversaries, found at first no retort to my adversaries' answers and then, when I replied, blamed me for having done so, because, according to them, no one had attacked me at all. While waiting, they will allow me to continue calling my adversaries my adversaries; for, despite the politeness of my century, I am rude like the Macedonians of Philip.

2. The disavowal of the Academy of Dijon on the subject of some writing falsely attributed by the Author to one of the members of this Academy can be seen in the *Mercure* of August 1752.

3. Every time that I think of my former simplicity, I cannot keep myself from laughing at it. I did not read a book of Morality or Philosophy without believing that I saw in it the soul and the principles of the Author. I looked upon all these serious writers as modest, wise, virtuous, irreproachable men. I formed from their trade angelic ideas, and I would only have approached one of their homes as if it were a sanctuary. In the end I saw them; this puerile prejudice dissipated, and this is the only error of which they have cured me.

4. When I say that our morals had been corrupted, I did not claim to say that those of our ancestors were good, but simply that ours were even worse. There are among men thousands of

sources of corruption; and though the pursuit of knowledge be perhaps the most abundant and most rapid, much is needed for it to be the only one. The fall of the Roman Empire, the invasions of a multitude of Barbarians, made a mix of all peoples, which must have necessarily destroyed the morals and customs of each of them. The Crusades, trade, the discovery of the Indies, navigation, long-distance travel, and still other causes that I wish not to cite, maintained and augmented disorder. All that facilitates communication between the diverse nations brings to some, not the virtues of others, but their crimes, and alters in all lands the morals that are unique to their climate and the constitution of their government. The pursuit of knowledge, therefore, did not do all the harm, just a good part of it; where it bore all the blame, is in having given to our vices an agreeable color, a certain air of honesty, which slows us from being horrified at it. When we first put on the play, *Le Méchant*, I remember that we found that the lead role did not correspond to the title. Cleon appeared to be but an ordinary man; he was, as was said, like everyone. This abominable scoundrel, whose character, once exposed, should have made all who have the misfortune of resembling him tremble within themselves, appeared to be a totally failed character whose darkness passed for kindness because those who believed themselves to be very honest men recognized themselves in him trait for trait.

5. Here is a modern example for those who reproach me for citing only ancient ones. The Republic of Genoa, looking to subjugate the Corsicans more easily, found no surer way than to establish an academy among them. It would not be difficult for me to lengthen this Note, but that would be an insult to the intelligence of the only Readers for whom I care.

6. I complain that Philosophy slackens the bonds of society that are formed by esteem and mutual goodwill, and I complain that the pursuit of knowledge, the arts, and all the other objects of commerce tighten the bonds of society through personal interest. Indeed, one of these bonds cannot be tightened without another one slackening in equal measure. There is therefore nothing contradictory in this.

7. I note that there currently reigns in this world a multitude of little maxims that seduce simpletons with a false air of philosophy, and which, besides that, are very convenient for ending disputes in an important and decisive tone, without needing to examine the question. Such is this one: "Men have the same passions everywhere; everywhere, self-love and self-interest direct them; therefore they are the same everywhere." When the Geometers made a supposition that, from reasoning to reasoning, leads them to an absurdity, they retrace their steps and demonstrate thus the supposition to be false. The same method applied to the maxim in question would easily show its absurdity: But let us reason in another way. A Savage is a man, and a European is a man. The half-philosopher instantly concludes that one is not worth more than the other, but the philosopher says: In Europe, government, laws, customs, interest, all place individuals in the necessity of cheating each other mutually and incessantly; all assign a duty of vice; they must be wicked to be wise, for there is absolutely no greater folly than to give the knaves their happiness at the expense of one's own. Among the Savages, personal interest speaks just as forcefully as among us, but it does not say the same things: Love of society and the care of their common defense are the only bonds that unite them:

This word of *propriety*, which costs so much crime in our honest people, has almost no meaning among them; they have no discussion among them of an interest that divides them; nothing brings them to cheat one another; public esteem is the only good to which each aspires and which they all deserve. It is very possible for a Savage to commit a bad deed, but it is not possible for him to make a habit of wrongdoing, for that would do him no good at all. I believe that we can make a very fair estimation of the morals of man upon the multitude of affairs that they have among them: The more they trade together, the more they admire their talents and their industry, the more they swindle each other decently and skillfully, and the more they are worthy of contempt. I say it with regret: The good man is he who has no need to cheat anyone, and the Savage is such a man.

> *Illum non populi fasces, non purpura Regum*
> *Flexit, et infidos agitans discordia fratres;*
> *Non res Romanæ, perituraque regna. Neque ille*
> *Aut doluit miserans inopem, aut invidit habenti.*[iv]

8. I find in history a unique, but striking example that seems to contradict this maxim: It is that of Rome's founding by a troop of bandits, whose descendants became in a few generations the most virtuous people that ever existed. I would have no trouble explaining this fact, if this were the place for it: But I will content myself with remarking that Rome's founders were less men whose morals had been corrupted, than men whose morals had not been at all formed: They did not scorn virtue, but neither did they know it yet; for these words *virtues* and *vices* are collective notions which are only born from frequenting men. Furthermore, it would be wrong to draw from this objection a conclusion in favor of the pursuit of knowledge; for of the first two

Kings of Rome who gave a form to the Republic and instituted its customs and its morals, one was in charge only of war, the other in charge only of sacred rites; the two things in the world farthest from Philosophy.

9. This simulacrum is a certain gentleness of morals that sometimes supplants their purity, a certain appearance of order that prevents horrible confusion, a certain admiration of beautiful things that prevents the good ones from falling completely into oblivion. It is the vice that takes the mask of virtue, not as hypocrisy in order to cheat and betray, but to remove itself under this lovable and sacred effigy from the horror that it has of itself when it sees itself uncovered.

10. I admire how much most people of Letters have been mistaken in this affair. When they saw the sciences and the arts attacked, they believed that they were personally being resented, while, without contradicting themselves, they could all think as I, that even though these things have done great harm to society, it is very essential to use them today as a medicine against the harm that they have caused, or as those malevolent animals which must be crushed as soon as they bite. In a word, there is not one man of Letters who, if he can bear that his behavior be examined according to the preceding article, could say in his favor what I say in mine; and this way of reasoning seems to me to suit them all the better for, between us, they care very little for the pursuit of knowledge, provided that it continues to bring honor to the learned. They are like the priests of paganism, who only adhered to religion as long as it made them respected.

TRANSLATOR'S NOTES TO THE PREFACE

i. The question to which Rousseau often refers was put forth by the Academy of Dijon as an essay contest in 1749, and asked, "Has the restoration of the sciences and arts contributed to the purification of morals?" Rousseau won this contest with his essay *The Discourse on the Moral Effects of the Arts & Sciences*.

ii. From Sallust's *Bellum Catilinæ*, Ch. 5, ❡ 1. The following translation comes from Sallust, Florus, & Velleius Paterculus, tr. by Rev. John Selby Watson (London: H. G. Bohn, 1852):

> *He had abundance of eloquence, though but little wisdom.*

iii. From Montaigne's *Essays*, Book III, Ch. 12 ("Of Physiognomy"). The translation in the text comes from Michel de Montaigne, *Complete Essays*, tr. by Donald M. Frame (California: Stanford University Press, 1958).

iv. From Virgil's *Georgics*, Book II, lines 495–496 and 498–499. The following translation comes from *The Georgics* of Virgil, tr. by Arthur S. Way (London: MacMillan & Co., 1912):

> *He stoops not to consuls' axes,*
> *he bows not to purple of kings,*
> *He recks not of hate that the hearts*
> *of faithless brethren wrings,*
> *Nor hath trembled for Rome's dark fortune,*
> *for empires nigh to their end.*
> *No poverty sees he to pity,*
> *no rich men to envy for aught.*

NARCISSUS,
OR
THE LOVER
OF HIMSELF,
A COMEDY

Played by les Comédiens ordinaires du Roi,
on 18 December 1752

DRAMATIS PERSONÆ

LISIMON

VALÈRE
LUCINDE } *Lisimon's children*

ANGELIQUE
LÉANDRE } *Brother & sister, Lisimon's wards*

MARTON, *Servant*

FRONTIN, *Valère's valet*

The play is set in Valère's apartment

SCENE 1

Lucinde, Marton

LUCINDE: I have just seen my brother walking in the garden. Let us hurry before he returns, & place the portrait on his dressing table.

MARTON: Here it is, Mademoiselle, so altered in its appearance as to make him unrecognizable. Though he's the prettiest man in the world, he shines here as a woman, but with a newfound elegance.

LUCINDE: Valère is, by his daintiness & the affectation of his fineries, a kind of woman in man's clothing, & this portrait so travestied seems less to disguise him than to return him to his natural state.

MARTON: And where's the harm in that? Since women today seek to draw themselves nearer to men, isn't it fitting that the latter meet them halfway and try to gain in allure as much as women do in resolve? Thanks to fashion, it'll be easier for everyone to find middle ground.

LUCINDE: I cannot approve of such ridiculous fashions. Perhaps our sex will have the good fortune not to be any less pleasant even as it becomes more esteemed. But as for men, I pity their blindness. What do these witless boys mean by usurping all of our rights? Do they hope to please women better by striving to look like them?

MARTON: If they did that, they'd be wrong, & women hate each other too much to love what looks like them. But let's get back to the portrait. Aren't you at all afraid that this little jest might upset the Chevalier?

LUCINDE: No, Marton, my brother is naturally good: He is even reasonable, almost to a fault. He will feel that in using this portrait to make a silent, playful reproach, I only thought of curing him of a petty fault that displeases even the tender Angelique, my father's amiable ward, whom Valère is to marry to-day. It is a service to her to correct her lover's faults, and you know how much I need the help of this dear friend to deliver me from Léandre, her brother, whom my father wishes me to wed.

MARTON: So this young stranger, this Cléonte that you saw last summer at Passy, is still dear to your heart?

LUCINDE: I do not deny it; in fact, I am counting on his word that he would come back soon, as well as on the promise that Angelique made to persuade her brother to give me up.

MARTON: Ah, give you up! Bear in mind that your eyes will have more power to seal this engagement than Angelique could ever have to break it.

LUCINDE: We will not debate your flattery; I will just tell you that as Léandre has never seen me, it will be easy for his sister to warn him, and to make him understand that, not being able to be happy with a woman whose heart is devoted to another, he could do no better than to free himself by way of an honest refusal.

MARTON: An honest refusal! Ah! Mademoiselle, refusing a woman with looks like yours, and forty thousand crowns to her name, that's an honesty of which Léandre will never be capable. (*Aside.*) If only she knew that Léandre and Cléonte were one and the same, such a refusal would take on quite a different meaning.

LUCINDE: Ah! Marton, I hear a sound; let us quickly hide the portrait. It is undoubtedly my brother coming back, and in distracting ourselves with gossip, we have deprived ourselves of the pleasure of carrying out our plan.

MARTON: No, it's Angelique.

SCENE II

Angelique, Lucinde, Marton

ANGELIQUE: My dear Lucinde, you know how reluctant I was to go along with your plan to have Valère's clothes in his portrait changed into women's finery. At present, as I see you ready to execute it, I fear that the displeasure of seeing himself made a fool will dispose him against us. Let us reconsider, I pray you, this frivolous jest. I feel that I can find no pleasure in making light of things if it means risking my heart's peace.

LUCINDE: How timid you are! Valère loves you too much to take offence at anything that comes from you, whilst you are still his mistress. Remember that you only have one day to breathe life into your fantasies, and that his own will come true all too soon. Moreover, it is a question of curing him of a foible that exposes him to mockery, and that is exactly a mistress's job. We can correct the faults of a lover. But, alas, we must put up with those of a husband.

ANGELIQUE: After all, what do you find so ridiculous in him? Since he is lovable, is he so wrong to love himself, and do we not set the example for him? He aims to please. Ah! If that is a fault, what more charming virtue could a man offer to society?

MARTON: Especially in the society of women.

ANGELIQUE: Finally, Lucinde, if you trust me, we will dispose of the portrait and this whole air of mockery, which could just as easily seem an insult as a correction.

LUCINDE: Oh! No. I will not lose the returns on my industry. But I am perfectly willing to run the risk alone, and nothing obliges you to be an accomplice in an affair to which you could be nothing more than a witness.

MARTON: What a beautiful distinction!

LUCINDE: I will enjoy seeing Valère's reaction. No matter how he takes it, it will still make for quite an amusing scene.

MARTON: I understand. The pretext is to correct Valère: But the real motive is to laugh at his expense. That's the genius and the delight of women. They often correct the ridiculous, only thinking to amuse themselves.

ANGELIQUE: Fine, if that is what you want, but I warn you that you will answer to me for the consequences.

LUCINDE: So be it.

ANGELIQUE: Since we have been together, you have crossed me a hundred times, for which I owe you punishment. If this affair causes me even the slightest annoyance with Valère, you had better watch out.

LUCINDE: Yes, yes.

ANGELIQUE: Give a little thought to Léandre.

LUCINDE: Ah! My dear Angelique ...

ANGELIQUE: Oh, if you cause me any trouble with your brother, I swear to you that you will marry mine. (*Aside.*) Marton, you have promised to keep the secret.

MARTON: (*Aside.*) Fear not.

LUCINDE: Finally, I ...

MARTON: I hear the Chevalier's voice. Make your decision as soon as possible, unless you want to give him a circle of girls around his dressing table.

LUCINDE: We have to avoid him seeing us. (*She places the portrait on his dressing table.*) There, the trap is set.

MARTON: I want to spy a little on my man to see …

LUCINDE: Silence. Let us get out of here.

ANGELIQUE: I fear that this will not end well.

SCENE III

Valère, Frontin

VALÈRE: Sangaride, today is a big day for you.

FRONTIN: Sangaride, or rather, Angelique. Yes, it's a big day: That of a wedding, and one that lengthens intolerably all the days that follow it.

VALÈRE: I am going to savor the pleasure of making Angelique happy!

FRONTIN: Would you desire to make her a widow?

VALÈRE: Oh, you wag... You know how much I love her. Tell me, to your knowledge, what could be missing from her happiness? With lots of love, a bit of wit, & a figure... such as you see, we can, I believe, always be rather sure to please.

FRONTIN: The thing's beyond doubt, and you've performed the first experiment on yourself.

VALÈRE: What I find a pity about it all, is that I do not know how many women my marriage will make dry up with regret, and who will no longer know what to do with their hearts.

FRONTIN: Oh, yes they will! Those women who have loved you, for example, will occupy themselves by loathing your better half. The others... But where the devil are we to find them, these others?

VALÈRE: The morning advances; it is time to get dressed to go and see Angelique. Let us go. (*He sits down at his dressing table.*) How do I look this morning? I do not have any sparkle in my eyes; my complexion looks weathered; I think I look so ordinary today.

FRONTIN: Ordinary! No, you're only at your level of ordinary.

VALÈRE: Using rouge is such a nasty habit; in the end, I will not be able to do without it, and in its absence, I will be all the worse for wear. Where then is my patch box? But what do I see here? A portrait... Ah! Frontin; what a charming object... Where did you get this portrait?

FRONTIN: Me? Hanged if I know what you're talking about.

VALÈRE: What! It was not you who put this portrait on my dressing table?

FRONTIN: Not on my life.

VALÈRE: Who would it be then?

FRONTIN: The truth is, I know nothing of the matter. It can only be the devil or you.

VALÈRE: Come off it. Someone has paid you off to keep silent... Do you know that comparison with this object wrongs Angelique? On my honor, this is the prettiest face that I have ever seen in my life. What eyes Frontin... I believe they resemble mine.

FRONTIN: That says everything.

VALÈRE: I find she has a look of me... She is, I must say, charming... Ah! If only she has the wits to match... But of course! Her taste answers for her mind. This minx is an expert on the finer things.

FRONTIN: What the devil! Let us see all these wonders.

VALÈRE: Look here. Do you think that you are fooling me with your simple-minded airs? Do you take me for a greenhorn in adventure?

FRONTIN: (*Aside.*) Am I not mistaken? It's him... it's himself. Look at him all decorated! What flowers!

What frills! This is Lucinde's doing; Marton will have done at least half of it. Let's not interfere in their mischief. My previous indiscretions have cost me too dearly.

VALÈRE: And so? Would Monsieur Frontin recognize this portrait's original?

FRONTIN: Humph! Of course I know her! Hundreds of kicks in the arse and as many slaps, which I had the singular honor of receiving, have cemented our acquaintance of each other.

VALÈRE: A girl who kicks! That's a bit saucy.

FRONTIN: She's simply prone to fits of impatience with her servants.

VALÈRE: How? Have you been in her employ?

FRONTIN: Yes, Monsieur; and I still have the honor of being her very humble servant.

VALÈRE: It would be rather amusing if there were a pretty woman in Paris whom I did not know! ... Tell me honestly. The original, is she as amiable as the portrait?

FRONTIN: Amiable? You know, Monsieur, if it were possible for someone to approach your own perfection, I could think of none more likely than she.

VALÈRE: (*Considering the portrait.*) My heart does not resist ... Frontin, tell me this beauty's name.

FRONTIN: (*Aside.*) Dear me, I've been caught off guard.

VALÈRE: What is her name? Speak.

FRONTIN: Her name is ... her name is ... she has no name. She is anonymous, like so many others.

VALÈRE: How depressingly suspicious this rascal is making me! Could it be that such charming traits were no more than those of a flirt?

FRONTIN: Why not? Beauty likes to adorn faces that only take pride in their beauty.

VALÈRE: What, she is ...

FRONTIN: A coquettish, simpering nobody whose vanity is without justification: In one word, a real tart.

VALÈRE: See how these knavish valets speak of the people that they have served. However, it must be seen. Tell me, where does she dwell?

FRONTIN: Oh, to dwell? Does such a one ever dwell?

VALÈRE: If you make me wait … Where does she lodge, you rascal?

FRONTIN: Good Lord, Monsieur, to be perfectly honest, your guess is as good as mine.

VALÈRE: How so?

FRONTIN: I swear to you that I know no better than you this portrait's original.

VALÈRE: It was not you who placed it there?

FRONTIN: No, may the plague suffocate me.

VALÈRE: These ideas that you gave me …

FRONTIN: Don't you see that you provide me with them yourself? Is there someone in the world as ridiculous as that?

VALÈRE: What! Am I to be unable to discover where this portrait comes from? The mystery and the challenge stoke my eagerness. For, I swear to you, I am really, very much in love with her.

FRONTIN: (*Aside.*) This is priceless! Look at him in love with himself.

VALÈRE: However, Angelique, the charming Angelique … In truth, I understand nothing of my heart, and I must see this new mistress before deciding anything about my marriage.

FRONTIN: What's that, Monsieur? You are not … Ah! You jest.

VALÈRE: No, I am telling you quite seriously that I cannot give my hand to Angelique, as long as the uncertainty of my feelings will be an obstacle to our mutual happiness. I cannot marry her today; the matter is settled.

FRONTIN: Yes, for you. But your father, who's already made his own resolutions, is the last man in the world to yield to yours; you know his weakness is not obliging others.

VALÈRE: She has to be found no matter the cost. Let us go, Frontin, run and search everywhere.

FRONTIN: Let's go, run, fly; let's take stock and make a report of all the pretty girls in Paris. Damn, what a fine work of literature that would be! A rare book, the reading of which would send no man to sleep!

VALÈRE: Let us make haste. Hurry and finish dressing me.

FRONTIN: Wait, here comes your father. Let's ask him to join us.

VALÈRE: Silence, tormentor. What an untimely obstacle.

SCENE IV

Lisimon, Valère, Frontin

LISIMON: (*Who must always have a brusque tone.*) And so, my son?

VALÈRE: Frontin, a chair for Monsieur.

LISIMON: I want to remain standing. I only have two words to say to you.

VALÈRE: I could only listen to you, Monsieur, if you were seated.

LISIMON: What a devil! He does not please me. You will see that this imp gives compliments to his father.

VALÈRE: Respect...

LISIMON: Oh! Respect consists of obeying me and doing nothing to get in my way. And what is this? Not dressed yet? On a wedding day? Isn't that nice! So, Angelique has not yet received your visit?

Valère: I was finishing my hair, and I was just about to dress to make myself presentable for her.

Lisimon: Are so many gadgets necessary just to do your hair and put some clothes on? By God, in my youth we used our time better, and without wasting three quarters of the day turning in circles before a mirror; we knew better how to advance our affairs with beautiful girls.

Valère: It seems to me, however, that if one wants to be loved, one can never take too much trouble in making oneself desirable, and that neglecting one's appearance is no way to demonstrate one's devotion to one's beloved.

Lisimon: Pure idiocy. A little bit of negligence is sometimes appropriate in love. Women took our enthusiasm more into account than the time we would have lost dressing in the morning; and, without affecting such delicacy in appearance, we had more in the heart. But let us change the subject. I thought to defer your marriage until Léandre's arrival, so that he might have the pleasure of attending, and I the pleasure of celebrating, your nuptials as well as your sister's on the same day.

Valère: (*Aside.*) Frontin, what luck!

FRONTIN: Yes, a marriage put off, that always means more time to repent.

LISIMON: What do you have to say about this, Valère? It seems that it would not be appropriate to marry the sister without waiting for the brother, since he is en route.

VALÈRE: I say, my father, that there is no better a thought.

LISIMON: This delay will cause you no pains then?

VALÈRE: The desire to obey you always overcomes any of my feelings of reluctance.

LISIMON: It was, however, from fear of upsetting you that I did not propose it to you.

VALÈRE: Your will is no less the ruler of my desires than of my actions. (*Aside.*) Frontin, how good a man my father is!

LISIMON: I am pleased to find you so docile; your reward will have cost you little; for, in a letter that I have just received, Léandre tells me that he is arriving today.

VALÈRE: And so, my father?

LISIMON: And so, my son, this way, nothing will have changed.

VALÈRE: How so? You would like to have him wedded upon arrival?

FRONTIN: Marry the man still in his riding boots!

LISIMON: No, not that; besides, since Lucinde and he have never met, they need a chance to get to know one another. But he will attend his sister's wedding, and I will not be so hard as to make such an obliging son as you languish.

VALÈRE: Monsieur…

LISIMON: Worry not; I know and approve of your hurry too well to play such a dirty trick on you.

VALÈRE: Father…

LISIMON: Let us leave it at that, I say; I already know what you are going to tell me.

VALÈRE: But Father… I'm having… thoughts…

LISIMON: You, thoughts? I was wrong. I would never have guessed that. On what then, if it please you, do your sublime meditations focus?

VALÈRE: On the inconveniences of marriage.

FRONTIN: That would be a rather lengthy text.

LISIMON: An idiot can sometimes think; but only after acting idiotically. Now I recognize my son.

VALÈRE: What do you mean, after acting idiotically? I am not yet married.

LISIMON: Learn, Monsieur the Philosopher, that there is no difference whatsoever between my will and action. You could have moralized when I made my proposal, yet you were so enthusiastic for it yourself. I would have willingly listened to your reasoning. For, you know how obliging I am.

FRONTIN: Oh! Yes Monsieur, we are, on that point, in a state to render justice unto you.

LISIMON: But now that all is at an end, you can speculate to your heart's content; it will, if you please, do no harm to the wedding.

VALÈRE: The constraint only strengthens my reluctance. Consider, I beseech you, the importance of the matter. Deign to give me a few days...

LISIMON: Adieu, my son; you will be married this night, or... you understand. (*Aside.*) As if I were duped by the hangdog's false whimper.

SCENE V

Valère, Frontin

VALÈRE: Heavens! How his obstinacy makes me suffer!

FRONTIN: Yes, married or disinherited! Wedded to a woman or to poverty! It's surely worth weighing the options.

VALÈRE: Me, weigh options! No; my choice was still uncertain; my father's intransigence has settled it.

FRONTIN: In favor of Angelique?

VALÈRE: Quite the contrary.

FRONTIN: I congratulate you, Monsieur, on such a heroic resolution. You're going to die of hunger as a worthy martyr for freedom. But if it were a matter of marrying the portrait? Hmm! Marriage would no longer seem so atrocious to you?

VALÈRE: No; but if my father desired to force me into it, I believe that I would resist with the same steadfastness, and I feel that my heart would bring me back to Angelique as soon as anyone sought to distance me from her.

FRONTIN: Such obedience! If you don't inherit the possessions of your father, you'll at least inherit his virtues. (*Looking at the portrait.*) Ah!

VALÈRE: What is it?

FRONTIN: Since our disgrace, this portrait seems to have taken on a rather starved appearance, a certain emaciated air.

VALÈRE: We have lost too much time to impertinence. We should have already covered half of Paris. (*He exits.*)

FRONTIN: At the rate that you're going, you'll soon have covered half the distance to Bedlam. Still, let's see how this all plays out; and as for me, to feign a search, I'd better start in a tavern.

SCENE VI

Angelique, Marton

MARTON: Ah! Ah, ah, ah! A pleasant scene! Who ever would have foreseen that? How much you've missed, Mademoiselle, by not hiding here with me to see him fall so deeply in love with his own charms!

ANGELIQUE: He saw himself through my eyes.

MARTON: What? You'd be so weak as to maintain your feelings for a man capable of such disloyalty?

ANGELIQUE: So he is guilty in your eyes! What have we, however, to reproach him with but the universal vice of his age? Still, do not believe that, unmoved by the Chevalier's insult, I will permit him to prefer to mine the first face that strikes him as agreeable. I love him too much not to be delicate, and Valère this day will sacrifice for me his folly, or I will sacrifice my love to my reason.

MARTON: I fear that one of those isn't as hard as the other.

ANGELIQUE: Here comes Lucinde. My brother must be arriving today. Take care that she does not suspect him to be her unknown admirer until the time is right.

SCENE VII

Lucinde, Angelique, Marton

MARTON: I'd wager, Mademoiselle, that you'd never guess the effect the portrait had? It'll surely make you laugh.

LUCINDE: Agh! Marton, let us drop the subject of the portrait; I have so many other things on my mind. My dear Angelique, I am sorry, I am dying. The moment has come when I need all the help you can give me. My father just told me of Léandre's arrival. He wants me to ready myself to receive him today and to give him my hand in a week.

ANGELIQUE: What do you find so terrible about that?

MARTON: How terrible indeed! Wanting to wed a beautiful girl of eighteen years to a rich and handsome man of twenty-two! It truly is the scariest of thoughts, and there isn't a single girl old enough to reason who wouldn't be feverish at the idea of such a marriage.

LUCINDE: I wish to hide nothing: I received, at the same time, a letter from Cléonte; he will shortly be in Paris; he will do something about my father; he implores me to put off my marriage: In the end, he still loves me. Ah, my dear, will you be unmoved by my fears despite this friendship you have sworn to me…

ANGELIQUE: The dearer this friendship is to me, the more I must wish to see our ties drawn closer through your marriage to my brother. However, Lucinde, your peace of mind is the first of my desires and my wishes accord with your own more than you think.

LUCINDE: Then deign to remember your promises. Make Léandre understand that my heart cannot be his, that…

MARTON: My God! Let's not swear anything. Men have such resources & women such inconstancy, that if Léandre were to get it into his head to charm you, I bet he'd succeed in spite of you.

LUCINDE: Marton!

MARTON: It won't even take him two days to replace your mystery man without leaving you the slightest regret.

LUCINDE: Let us go on ... Dear Angelique, I count on your care; and in my troubled state, I am frantically trying everything to have my father delay, if possible, a marriage that my heart makes me contemplate with dread. (*She exits.*)

ANGELIQUE: I should stop her. But Lisimon is not a man to yield to his daughter's pleas, and all of her prayers will only strengthen this marriage that she herself wants, all the more so as she seems to fear it. If it pleases me to take advantage of her worries for a few moments, it is to make the end result sweeter for her. What other vengeance could friendship permit?

MARTON: I'm going to follow her and, without betraying our secret, prevent her, if possible, from doing something foolish.

SCENE VIII

Angelique

ANGELIQUE: How foolish I am! My mind busies itself with trifles while I have so many affairs of the
heart to attend to. Alas! Perhaps at this very moment Valère is proving his infidelity. Perhaps, aware
of all and ashamed at having let himself be caught
unawares, he is giving his heart to some other object
out of spite. Such are men; they never venge themselves with more passion than when they are most
wrong. But here he comes, wrapped up in his portrait.

SCENE IX

Angelique, Valère

VALÈRE: (*Without seeing Angelique.*) I race without knowing where to look for this charming object. Will love not guide my feet at all?

ANGELIQUE: (*Aside.*) Ingrate! It guides them only too well.

VALÈRE: Such is love, always with its burdens. I must bear them while seeking this beauty that I love, not being able to find any other that makes me love.

ANGELIQUE: (*Aside.*) What impertinence! Alas! How can one be so vain and so lovable at the same time?

VALÈRE: I must wait for Frontin: He may have had more luck. In any case, Angelique adores me…

ANGELIQUE: (*Aside.*) What treachery! You know my weakness too well.

VALÈRE: After all, I still feel that I will not lose what I have: her heart, her charms, all is there.

ANGELIQUE: (*Aside.*) It will be an honor for me to be his consolation prize.

VALÈRE: What strangeness afflicts my bosom! I am renouncing possession of a charming object to which, at bottom, my feelings continue to attract me. I am exposing myself to my father's displeasure by losing my head over a beautiful woman, perhaps unworthy of my sighs, perhaps not even real, because of nothing more than a portrait that has appeared out of nowhere and that is certainly better looking than reality. What caprice! What folly! And yet! Folly and caprice, are they not the distinguishing marks of a loveable man? (*Looks at portrait.*) What grace! … What features! … How enchanted! … How divine! Ah! May Angelique not flatter herself by trying to compare herself to such charms.

ANGELIQUE: (*Seizing the portrait.*) I assuredly will keep myself from doing so. But may I be allowed to share your admiration? Knowledge of this favored rival's charms will at least lighten the shame of my defeat.

VALÈRE: Heavens!

ANGELIQUE: What is the matter? You appear dumb-founded. I would never have believed that a dandy could be so easily unnerved.

VALÈRE: Ah! Cruel woman, you know all the influence you have over me, and you insult me without letting me answer.

ANGELIQUE: I admit that was very poorly done on my part; and you should have the right to insult me. Go, Chevalier, I pity your embarrassment. Here is your portrait; I am so much the less angry that you love its original since your feelings on the matter are exactly the same as mine.

VALÈRE: What! You know this person?

ANGELIQUE: Not only do I know her, but I can also tell you that she is the most valuable thing I have in the world.

VALÈRE: Truly, that is news, and the language strikes me as rather strange coming from the mouth of a rival.

ANGELIQUE: I do not know! But it is sincere. (*Aside.*) If he becomes vexed, I win.

VALÈRE: So does she have any merit?

ANGELIQUE: She alone has it infinitely.

VALÈRE: And is without fault, no doubt?

ANGELIQUE: Oh! Many. She is a petty, bizarre, capricious, vapid, giddy, flighty, & above all intolerably vain person. And yet! She is lovable even with all that, and I predict that you will love her to the grave.

VALÈRE: You give your consent then?

ANGELIQUE: Yes.

VALÈRE: You will not be angry in the slightest?

ANGELIQUE: No.

VALÈRE: (*Aside.*) I despair at her indifference. (*Aloud.*) Dare I flatter myself by asking you to strengthen your union with her on my behalf?

ANGELIQUE: It is all that I ask.

VALÈRE: (*Irritated.*) You say all of this with a calm that bewitches me.

ANGELIQUE: How so? You were just complaining about my cheerfulness, and now you are upset by my composure. I do not know what tone to take with you.

VALÈRE: (*Aside.*) I am dying of spite. (*Aloud.*) Will Mademoiselle do me the honor of introducing me to her?

ANGELIQUE: That, for example, is the kind of service that I am quite sure you were not expecting of me: But I want to exceed your hopes, and once again I promise you that I will do it.

VALÈRE: Will it be soon at least?

ANGELIQUE: Perhaps as soon as today.

VALÈRE: I cannot wait any longer. (*He wants to go.*)

ANGELIQUE: (*Aside.*) I am beginning to foresee a favorable end to all of this; he has too much spite not to have any more love. (*Aloud.*) Where are you going, Valère?

VALÈRE: I see that my presence makes you uncomfortable and I yield the place to you.

ANGELIQUE: Ah! Not at all. I will leave myself: It is not right that I force you to leave your own place.

VALÈRE: Go, go; remember that he who loves nothing does not deserve to be loved.

ANGELIQUE: It is still worth more to love nothing than to be in love with oneself.

SCENE X

Valère

VALÈRE: In love with oneself! Is it a crime to have some sense of one's worth? I am still quite stung. Is it possible to lose a lover such as I without any pain? One would say that she looks upon me as an ordinary man. Alas! I hide in vain the trouble of my heart, and I tremble at loving her again after her inconstancy. But no; my heart belongs to this charming object alone. Let us hurry and commence the search anew; and let us combine the task of making myself happy with that of arousing Angelique's jealousy. But here's Frontin.

SCENE XI

Valère, Frontin (drunk)

FRONTIN: What the devil! I don't know why I can't stand; especially when I tried my best to gather my strength.

VALÈRE: Very well, Frontin, did you find...?

FRONTIN: Oh! Yes, Monsieur.

VALÈRE: Ah? Heavens, could it be?

FRONTIN: Also, I had quite a lot of trouble.

VALÈRE: Hurry up and tell me...

FRONTIN: I had to check all the taverns in the neighborhood.

VALÈRE: Taverns!

FRONTIN: But my success surpassed my hopes.

VALÈRE: Tell me then …

FRONTIN: It was a fire … A froth …

VALÈRE: What the devil is this animal mumbling about?

FRONTIN: Wait for me to get everything in the right
order.

VALÈRE: Shut up, you drunken rascal; or speak to me of
the orders that I gave you concerning the portrait's
original.

FRONTIN: Ah! Yes, the original. Exactly. Rejoice, rejoice,
I tell you!

VALÈRE: What for?

FRONTIN: She's not at the White Cross, nor the Gold
Lion, nor the Pinecone, nor …

VALÈRE: Tormentor, will you finish?

FRONTIN: Patience. Since she's not there, she must be
elsewhere; and … oh, I'll find her, I'll find her …

VALÈRE: I am just itching to knock him out. Let us leave.

SCENE XII

Frontin

FRONTIN: Here I am, a rather pretty boy... This floor is devilishly uneven. Where was I? Oh my, I'm no longer there. Ah! If I...

SCENE XIII

Lucinde, Frontin

LUCINDE: Frontin, where is your master?

FRONTIN: I think at the moment he's looking for himself.

LUCINDE: How so, looking for himself?

FRONTIN: Yes, he's looking for himself to marry himself.

LUCINDE: But what is all this gibberish?

FRONTIN: This gibberish! Then you understand nothing of it?

LUCINDE: No, in truth.

FRONTIN: Oh Lord, me neither: Still, I'll explain it to you, if you so wish.

LUCINDE: How are you going to explain to me that which you do not understand?

FRONTIN: Oh! Lady, I've done my studies.

LUCINDE: He's drunk, I believe. Ho! Frontin, I beseech
you, recall a bit of your common sense; try to make
yourself understood.

FRONTIN: Of course, nothing could be easier. Hold this.
It's a portrait … metamor … no, metaphore … yes,
metaphorized. This is my master, this is a girl … you
did a bit of mixing … I guessed all of that. And so,
can we speak more clearly?

LUCINDE: No, that is not possible.

FRONTIN: Only my master understands nothing of it.
For he's fallen in love with his own image.

LUCINDE: What! Without recognizing himself?

FRONTIN: Yes, & that's exactly what's so extraordinary.

LUCINDE: Ah! I understand everything else. And who
could have foreseen that? Run quickly, my poor
Frontin, fly to find your master and tell him that I
have the most pressing of matters to discuss with
him. Take care, above all, not to mention a word to
him of what you have guessed. Here, this is for …

FRONTIN: For drinking, right?

LUCINDE: Oh no, you've had quite enough.

FRONTIN: Better safe than sorry.

SCENE XIV

Lucinde

LUCINDE: Let us not falter for an instant, let us face it;
and whatever may happen to me because of it, let us
not suffer such a dear brother to make a fool of himself by the very means I had employed to correct his
folly. How miserable I am! I have inconvenienced
my brother; my father, irritated by my resistance,
has become even more of a despot; my absent lover
is in no position to come to my aid; I fear the betrayal of a friend, and the careful planning of a man
that I cannot bear: For I surely hate him. I feel as if
I would prefer death to being with Léandre.

SCENE XV

Angelique, Lucinde, Marton

ANGELIQUE: Console yourself, Lucinde, Léandre does not wish to bring about your death. I admit, however, that he did want to see you without your knowing it.

LUCINDE: Alas! So much the worse.

ANGELIQUE: Are you aware that your "so much the worse" is not the most unpretentious thing you've ever said?

MARTON: It's a little vein of fraternal blood.

LUCINDE: My God, how nasty you both are! So, what did he say after that?

ANGELIQUE: He told me that he would be in despair if he obtained you against your will.

MARTON: Of course, he did add that your resistance pleased him in some way. But he said that with a certain air ... Do you know that if I had to judge your feelings for him, I'd wager that he is not to be outdone by you. Hate him as much as you like, he will pay you back in kind.

LUCINDE: So much for politely obeying me.

MARTON: To treat us women politely, a man mustn't always bend his will to ours.

ANGELIQUE: He has agreed to give you up, if only you will receive him so he can bid you farewell.

LUCINDE: Oh, no; I shall relieve him of that duty.

ANGELIQUE: Ah! You cannot refuse him that. It is, in any case, a commitment that I made to him. I give you fair warning that he is resting high hopes on the success of this meeting, and that he dares to hope that after appearing before your eyes, you will no longer resist this union.

LUCINDE: He is quite the braggart then.

MARTON: His boast is that he'll tame you.

ANGELIQUE: And it is through this hope alone that he consented to what I proposed to him.

MARTON: I'm informing you that he's only accepting the arrangement because he's quite sure that you'll not take him at his word.

LUCINDE: How unbearably smug he must be. Very well, he only needs to show up: I will be curious to see how he plans to win me over, and I give you my word that he will be received with an air … Let him come. He needs a lesson; count on him receiving … an instructive one.

ANGELIQUE: Look at yourself, my dear Lucinde; we do not keep all the promises we make ourselves; I'd wager that you will relent.

MARTON: You'll see that men are excessively skilled; your every wish will be fulfilled.

LUCINDE: You may be assured of that.

ANGELIQUE: Just beware: You won't say that we did not warn you.

MARTON: It won't be our fault if he surprises you.

LUCINDE: I honestly believe that you want to drive me mad.

ANGELIQUE: (*Aside to Marton.*) She's right about something. (*Aloud.*) If that is your desire, Marton will bring him to you.

LUCINDE: What?

MARTON: We left him in the antechamber; he will be here in an instant.

LUCINDE: O dear Cléonte! May you not see how I receive your rivals!

SCENE XVI

Angelique, Lucinde, Marton, Léandre

ANGELIQUE: Approach, Léandre, and teach Lucinde to know her own heart better; she believes that she hates you, and will make every effort to receive you poorly: But I tell you that all of these apparent marks of hatred are in fact the truest proofs of love.

LUCINDE: (*Still without looking at Léandre.*) If that's the case, I assure you, the poor simpleton may think himself quite adored.

ANGELIQUE: Come now, Lucinde, must your anger prevent you from looking at people?

LÉANDRE: If my love is guilty of arousing your hatred, behold the most despised criminal of them all. (*He throws himself at Lucinde's knees.*)

LUCINDE: Cléonte! Ah, wicked Angelique!

LÉANDRE: Léandre displeased you so much that I dared not, under that name, avail myself of the favor that

I received under that of Cléonte. But if the purpose of my disguise may justify its effect, you will forgive the delicacy of a heart whose weakness is the desire to be loved for being itself.

LUCINDE: Stand up, Léandre; an excess of delicacy only offends those hearts that lack it, and mine is as happy with the trial as yours must be with its success. But you, Angelique! Was my dear Angelique cruel enough to amuse herself with my troubles?

ANGELIQUE: Oh, now's a fine time to start complaining! You are both happy, while I, alas, am beset by anxiety.

LÉANDRE: What? My dear sister, you were thinking about my happiness, even while you were worried about your own. Ah! That is a kindness which I will never forget. (*He kisses her hand.*)

SCENE XVII

Léandre, Valère, Angelique, Lucinde, Marton

VALÈRE: Let not my presence disturb you. What's this, Mademoiselle? I neither knew of all your conquests, nor of the fortunate object of your preference, and I will take care to remember humbly that, having loved the most constantly, Valère was the most ill treated.

ANGELIQUE: Loved the most constantly? Ill-treated? Better it were so, than to suffer the reality of your inconstancy. You could certainly use some lessons in modesty.

VALÈRE: What? You dare join mockery to insult and you have the effrontery to applaud yourself when you should die of shame?

ANGELIQUE: Ah! You are getting angry. I am leaving; I do not like being insulted.

VALÈRE: No, you will stay; I shall enjoy your embarrassment.

ANGELIQUE: Well then, enjoy yourself.

VALÈRE: For I hope that you will not be so bold as to justify yourself.

ANGELIQUE: Have no fear.

VALÈRE: And do not flatter yourself with the idea that I still retain the slightest of feelings towards you.

ANGELIQUE: My opinion of that will change nothing of the matter.

VALÈRE: At this point, I have nothing for you but hatred.

ANGELIQUE: Kindly spoken.

VALÈRE: (*Taking the portrait.*) And behold, henceforth, the only object of my love.

ANGELIQUE: You are right. And I declare that I have for Monsieur (*Pointing to her brother.*) an attachment that is hardly inferior to yours for the portrait's original.

VALÈRE: Ingrate! Alas, I have nothing left to do but die.

ANGELIQUE: Valère, listen. I pity the state in which I see you. You must agree that you are the most unjust of men, to let yourself get carried away by an appearance of infidelity for which you, yourself, gave me the model; but even now, my heart impels me to overlook your failings.

VALÈRE: You will see that I have the honor of being forgiven!

ANGELIQUE: In truth, you hardly deserve it. Let me, however, explain to you the price of my forgiveness. You have, so far, borne witness to me of feelings that I repaid with a return too tender for such an ingrate. Despite that, you have disgracefully insulted me by a ludicrous love for a simple portrait with all the lightness and, dare I say, thoughtlessness of your age and character. It is not a matter of accusing me of having behaved like you; nor is it for you, who are guilty, to condemn my conduct.

VALÈRE: Not for me, great Gods! But let us see where this fine speech leads to.

ANGELIQUE: Here it is. I told you that I knew the object of your new love and that is true. I added that I loved her tenderly and that is also too true. By admitting to you her worth, I did nothing to disguise her faults. Moreover, I promised to introduce you to her & I shall make good on my word to do so this very day, even this very hour: For I warn you that she is closer to you than you think.

VALÈRE: What's this?

ANGELIQUE: Do not interrupt me, I beg of you. At last, the truth forces me to repeat to you that this person loves you ardently, and I can tell you of her attachment as if it were my own. It is now for you to choose, between her and me, the one to whom you will give all your tenderness: Choose, Chevalier, but choose this very instant & do not look back.

MARTON: Look at that, I believe he's embarrassed. The alternative is pleasant. Believe me, Monsieur, choose the portrait; it's the way to be protected from your rivals.

LUCINDE: Ah! Valère, must you waver for so long before following the inclinations of your heart?

VALÈRE: (*At Angelique's feet & tossing the portrait aside.*) It is done; you have won, beautiful Angelique, & I feel how much the feelings born of caprice are inferior to those that you inspire. (*Marton picks up the portrait.*) But, alas! When all my heart returns to you, may I flatter myself by saying that it will bring yours back to me?

ANGELIQUE: You will be able to judge my gratitude by
the sacrifice you have just made for me. Stand up,
Valère, & look carefully at these features.

LÉANDRE: (*Also looking.*) Wait a minute! But I believe
that I recognize this object ... It is ... yes, I believe,
it is him ...

VALÈRE: Who, him? Say rather her. It is a woman that
I renounce, like all the women of the universe, over
whom Angelique will always carry the day.

ANGELIQUE: Yes, Valère; perhaps a woman until now:
But I hope that he will henceforth be a man superior
to these petty weaknesses which degraded his sex
and character.

VALÈRE: You have cast me into the queerest of surprises!

ANGELIQUE: You ought to recognize this object with
which you had the most intimate commerce, and
which assuredly no one will accuse you of having
neglected. Remove from its head the strange adorn-
ment that your sister had added to it ...

VALÈRE: Ah! What do I see?

MARTON: The thing isn't clear? You see the portrait;
look at the original.

VALÈRE: Oh heavens! May I not die of shame!

MARTON: Eh, Monsieur, you're perhaps the only one of your order who might have known what shame was.

ANGELIQUE: Ingrate! Was I wrong to tell you that I loved this portrait's original?

VALÈRE: And I want to continue loving him only because he adores you.

ANGELIQUE: In order to strengthen our reconciliation, please let me introduce to you Léandre, my brother.

LÉANDRE: Allow me, Monsieur …

VALÈRE: Gods! What height of bliss! What! Even when I was an ingrate, Angelique was not unfaithful?

LUCINDE: May I take part in your happiness! And may my own be increased because of it.

SCENE XVIII

Lisimon, the characters from the previous scene

LISIMON: Ah! Look at all of you gathered together so conveniently. As Valère and Lucinde had both shown such resistance, I had at first resolved to constrain them to their marriages. But I came to the conclusion that it is sometimes necessary to be a good father, and that violence does not always make for happy marriages. I therefore made the decision to break off this day all that had been decreed; and here are the new arrangements, which take their stead: Angelique will marry me; Lucinde will go to a convent; Valère will be disinherited; and as for you, Léandre, you will just have to exercise patience.

MARTON: Nicely done, I say! This is fairly measured; we could do no better.

LISIMON: What's the matter? You all look dumbfounded! Does this plan not suit your tastes?

MARTON: Who will be the first to open his mouth? The pestilence of stupid lovers & stupid youth whose useless prattle never ceases, and who don't know how to find the right word when it's necessary!

LISIMON: Let us go, you know my intentions. You only have to conform to them.

LÉANDRE: Ah, Monsieur! Deign to suspend your wrath. Do you not read the repentance of the guilty in their eyes & their discomfort, and do you want to make the mistake of subjecting the innocent to the same punishment?

LISIMON: I would like to indulge myself by testing their obedience one last time. Let us see a little. So, Monsieur Valère, do you still have your thoughts?

VALÈRE: Yes, my father; but instead of the troubles of marriage, they offer me nothing more than its pleasures.

LISIMON: Oh, oh! You have indeed changed your language! And you, Lucinde, do you still love your freedom?

LUCINDE: I feel, my father, that it may be sweet to lose it under the laws of duty.

LISIMON: Ah, look at them all so reasonable. I am charmed. Kiss me, my children, and let us go and conclude these happy unions. How a bit of authority can strike so opportunely!

VALÈRE: Come, beautiful Angelique; you have cured me of a ridicule that was the shame of my youth; and I will henceforth prove with you that when one loves truly, one no longer thinks of oneself.

The End

AFTERWORD

Theater is Narcissism:
On Jean-Jacques Rousseau's *Narcisse*[1]

SIMON CRITCHLEY

What is the connection between narcissism and inequality? For Rousseau, the great sea change in the history of inequality is the institution of private property, where someone said "'this is mine' and found people simple enough to believe him."[2] Yet, even prior to the establishment of private property, when human beings first gathered together, socialized, and looked at one another — Rousseau imagines this taking place around a tree in a purported state of nature, and the notion of the look, the narcissistic *regard*, is essential — there was engendered a desire for distinction, to be distinct and different from the others. It is with this desire for distinction

---

1. This text was originally prepared as part of a series of events to mark the bicentenary of Schiller's death entitled *Spieltrieb. Was bringt die Klassik auf die Bühne? (Playdrive. What Brings the Classics to the Stage?)*, held in Weimar in November 2005. It was originally published in German as "Theater ist Narzissmus — Über Jean-Jacques Rousseaus „Narziss"," *Theater der Zeit*, Heft № 10 (October 2005) 144–153.

2. Jean-Jacques Rousseau, *The Basic Political Writings*, tr. & ed. by Donald A. Cess (Indiana: Hackett, 2011) 69.

that the healthy *amour de soi* or self-love that defines human beings in a natural state begins to be transformed into a narcissistic *amour propre* or pride. For Rousseau, the origin of narcissism consists in this desire for social distinction, from a sense of one's own importance. Thus, inequality and narcissism derive from the same source.

This is the kernel of the drama that is played out in *Narcisse, ou l'amant de lui-même*. Rousseau wrote seven plays, in various stages of completion or incompletion. *Narcisse* was the only one to be performed publicly — and even then, it received only a single performance, by *Les comédiens du Roi*, on December 18, 1752. *Narcisse* found its way to the stage because of the considerable success of *Le Devin du village*, Rousseau's one-act pastoral opera, which had been performed before the French King, Queen, and court at Fontainebleau the previous October. Louis XV was so impressed by the play that he requested to have an audience with Rousseau, but Rousseau was so neurotically plagued by a weak bladder that he was panicked that he would wet himself during the audience and he therefore declined, complaining of his '*infirmités*.'

Narcisse was described by Rousseau's sometime friend Grimm as '*une mauvaise comédie*,' and although one might expect more loyalty from a friend, he is not incorrect in his judgment. The play is in the style of Marivaux, who read, commented, and even made some changes to the text. Sadly, *Narcisse* is not equal in quality to Marivaux's plays, which is perhaps explained by the fact that Rousseau claimed in the *Confessions* to have written the play when he was just 18 years old. This, though, is certainly not the whole truth: it is clear that Rousseau periodically and significantly redrafted the play between his youth and the time of its only performance, when Rousseau was 40. Indeed, he admits as much in the *Confessions*: "when I stated in the preface to that play that I had written it at eighteen I lied to the extent of some years."[3] Nonetheless, it is probable that *Narcisse* was Rousseau's first extended piece of literary composition.

The action of *Narcisse* is very simple. It concerns a man, Valère, who falls in love with a painting of himself dressed as a woman. The drama begins with Valère's sister, Lucinde, devising a plan to trick the incurably vain protagonist, who is engaged to be married to Angelique. The trick is to test his love for her, something which backfires horribly as Valère falls completely in love with his own feminized portrait, his objectified self-image. There is much playful,

3. Jean-Jacques Rousseau, *The Confessions*, tr. by J.M. Cohen (London: Penguin, 1953) 119.

if predictable, dramatic irony, when Valère sends off his man, Frontin, in search all over Paris for his new beloved, who is in fact himself.

> LUCINDE: Frontin, where is your master?
> FRONTIN: I think at the moment he's looking for himself.
> LUCINDE: How so, looking for himself?
> FRONTIN: Yes, he's looking for himself to be married to himself. (40)

Eventually Valère realizes his mistake & the error of his ways, is scolded by his father, and decides to marry Angelique after all. There is also a second love story in *Narcisse*, which is curiously unresolved and unsatisfactorily presented in the play, between Lucinde & Léandre, which mirrors the main dramatic relationship.

The play is then a lesson in the failings of narcissism that ends with a moral: "when one loves truly, one no longer thinks of oneself" (58). As such, it is a derivative, slight, and nicely inconsequential piece, just the sort of thing that Rousseau thought might gain him some sort of a literary reputation when he moved to Paris in 1742, in his thirtieth year.

However, matters become more compelling when the play is read alongside the long preface that Rousseau wrote to accompany its publication in 1752.

In his *Confessions*, Rousseau declares that the preface is "one of my best pieces of writing."[4] In this way the play is situated between the arguments of Rousseau's First & Second Discourses, in 1750 & 1755. Allow me to rehearse the philosophical arguments here by recounting a famous anecdote, that of Rousseau's moment of 'illumination.' In 1749, when Rousseau was 37 years old, he went to see his friend and fellow encyclopaedist Denis Diderot, who at that time was imprisoned at Vincennes outside Paris, for expressing opinions contrary to religion and the state. Short of money, Rousseau used to walk the 5 miles to the prison and to entertain himself on the journey would read a journal or newspaper. On one occasion, reading the literary gazette *Mercure de France*, he came across a subject proposed by the Academy of Dijon for an essay competition: "Has the progress in the arts and sciences done more to corrupt or to purify morals?" In a sudden flash, akin to the vision of Paul on the road to Damascus, Rousseau realized that progress in the arts and sciences had, in fact, corrupted morals. In a letter to Malesherbes from 1762, Rousseau writes of this experience, with a characteristic absence of emotional overstatement:

---

4. Ibid., 361.

If ever anything resembled a sudden inspiration, it is what that advertisement stimulated in me: all at once I felt my mind dazzled by a thousand lights, a crown of splendid ideas presented themselves to me with such force and in such confusion, that I was thrown into a state of indescribable bewilderment. I felt my head seized by a dizziness that resembled intoxication. A violent palpitation constricted me and made my chest heave. Unable to breathe and walk at the same time, I sank down under one of the trees in the avenue and passed the next half hour in such agitation that when I got up I found that the front of my jacket was wet with tears, although I had no memory of shedding any. Ah, Monsieur, if ever I had been able to write down what I saw and felt as I sat under that tree, with what clarity would I have exposed the contradictions of our social system, with what force would I have demonstrated all the abuses of our institutions, with what simplicity would I have demonstrated that man is naturally good, and has only become bad because of those institutions.[5]

---

5. Quoted in Maurice Cranston, *Jean-Jacques: The Early Life & Work of Jean-Jacques Rousseau* (Chicago: University of Chicago Press, 1982) 228.

The central belief of what is all too glibly called
the Enlightenment, which derives from Bacon and
which is absolutely decisive for figures like Voltaire
and Diderot, is the belief in progress. That is to say,
the development of science, technology, art, and culture has led to the amelioration of humanity — or,
in Kant's formulation, Enlightenment is freedom
from man's self-incurred tutelage. For Rousseau,
on the contrary, rational and scientific progress is
moral and political regress. Civilization is decline.
The so-called progress in the arts and sciences has
made humanity worse: less human, more depraved,
selfish, and greedy. What we see in Rousseau is an
early version of 19th-Century theories of history, in
particular that of Marx and Engels in *The German
Ideology* and the opening pages of *The Communist
Manifesto*, where the seeming progress of humanity
has led to progressive alienation from our true condition, what the young Marx called "species-being."
But we equally see an anticipation of Nietzschean
genealogy in Rousseau, where the history of morality is the crushing of the active forces of life-affirma-
tion by the cringing *ressentiment* of Judeo-Christian
morality. For Rousseau, human history, society, and
so-called civilization have all conspired to the degra-
dation of the human condition: man was born free,
but he is everywhere enchained.

However, if such is Rousseau's position, then isn't it utterly hypocritical of him to publish and indeed permit the performance of a play like *Narcisse*, not to mention his more or less successful experiments with opera, ballet, music, and poetry? Betraying early signs of the paranoia that would painfully suffocate him in later life, seeing spies at every turn, Rousseau spends much of the preface responding polemically to this objection. First comes his implausible claim that *Narcisse* is merely a work of his youth and shouldn't be taken seriously. Secondly, and more compellingly, he argues that given that Parisian society is so utterly and irredeemably corrupt in regard to morals (*les mœurs*), it is better to divert them with such trifles as the theater, as this might prevent them from engaging in more harmful, wicked activities like violence & warfare. "Thus I suggest," he continues with caustic irony,

> and I have already said this more than once, that we allow the existence & even the careful maintenance of the Academies, Colleges, Universities, Libraries, Spectacles, and all other amusements that can make some sort of diversion for the wickedness of men, & prevent them from occupying their idleness with more dangerous things. For in a country where it would no longer be a question of honest people &

good morals, it would still be better to live with rascals than with brigands.[6]

From this perspective, the failure of *Narcisse* to extend beyond its opening performance offers Rousseau a rather perverse vindication of his views. He writes, with some delight:

> My play had the fate it deserved and that I had foreseen; but, despite the near annoyance that it caused me, I left the performance much happier with myself, and more rightfully so than if it had been a success.[7]

Thus, the manifest failure of *Narcisse* is transformed into success and its mediocre tediousness is an inverted triumph for Rousseau's assault on culture.

If we place *Narcisse* in the context of Rousseau's arguments in the preface and *Discourses*, then the question of narcissism takes on a rather different, deeper aspect. If narcissism is the experiential effect of inequality — or rather its lived affect — then the very idea of theater is thereby condemned. This becomes clear if *Narcisse* is linked to the *Letter to D'Alembert*, where Rousseau denounces D'Alembert's proposal for a theater in Geneva.

---

6. Rousseau, *Œuvres complètes*, Tome 2, 972. See p. xviii of this edition.

7. Ibid., 973. See p. xx of this edition.

Rousseau makes two main accusations against theater. First, he says theater is morally and socially dangerous because it reverses the purportedly natural relation between the sexes, permitting women to take power over men through the play of theatrical representation. Theater — and here Rousseau is thinking of the playful comic ironies of Molière — reverses the hierarchy of the sexes and is essentially effeminizing. Seen in this light, the travesty of *Narcisse*, where the male protagonist falls in love with his own cross-dressed feminized image, enacts the entire sexual threat of theater.

The secondly strand of Rousseau's critique concerns representation. In it, he restates Plato's critique of the tragic poets in the *Republic* where theater is excluded from the well-ordered *polis* because it is the *mimesis* or imitation of a mere appearance rather than an attention to the true form of things which should be the proper concern of the philosopher.

This critique of theater as feminization and representation runs together with his proposal to replace theater with civic spectacles, an idea that had a direct influence on Robespierre's *fêtes nationales civiques* in the years after the French Revolution. What is essential to such spectacles is that they are not representations but the presence to itself of the people coming together outdoors in daylight and not lingering in the darkness of the theater, whose very architecture, says Rousseau, is reminiscent of Plato's cave:

> Plant a stake crowned with flowers in the middle of a square, gather the people together there, and you will have a festival. Do better yet; let the spectators become an entertainment to themselves; make them actors themselves; do it so that each see and loves himself in the others so that all will be better united.[8]

In the civic spectacle, the people do not passively watch a theatrical object of representation, but rather become the self-present subject of their own drama, the enactors of their own sovereignty. This idea obviously has enormous political significance & it is clear that behind the condemnation of theater stands a radical critique of a decadent political system. Rousseau's defense of popular sovereignty in *The Social Contract* is of a piece with his critique of any and all forms of representative government. The only way of attaining political legitimacy, and balancing the seemingly opposed claims of freedom and equality, is to root sovereignty in the will of the people — not in some external authority, such as a monarch or a hereditary aristocracy.

---

8. Ibid., 126.

The people should be the actors in the theater of the state. If one bears this in mind, then the festival becomes the lived manifestation of popular sovereignty, the reinforcement of the people's individual and collective autonomy.

The civic festival is the enacting of the general will without the mediation of representation. As such, Rousseau's idea of the civic festival finds a powerful echo in Schiller's conception of the æsthetic revolution that must accompany any political revolution, a vision that finds its most dramatic and aphoristic expression, as Jacques Rancière shows, in the sensuous political organicism of the *Oldest System-Program of German Idealism* and its call for a "new mythology."[9] By contrast, the theater is a veritable temple to Narcissus, a cavernous hall of mirrors that reflects nothing more than the desire for distinction and the hypocrisy of *amour propre*. The theater is a place where actors are not subjects, but objectify themselves in their desire to see and be seen. Theater is the very crucible of narcissism *&* inequality.

All of which means that the status of Rousseau's theater is peculiar, perhaps without precedent, though with many subsequent imitators: *it is theater*

9. Jacques Rancière, "Schiller et la promesse esthétique," *Europe. Revue littéraire mensuelle* (April 2014) 7–21.

against theater; it is theater against the very idea of theatricality. What is theater? It is narcissism. What is theater for? It allows human beings to experience their cave-like captivity in the order of representation *&* objectification and to become alienated from their true subjectivity, both individual and communal. What, then, might be the purpose of Rousseau's theater? It is nothing less than a means for diagnosing and criticizing the essential narcissism of modernity and subverting its drama of inequality. Theater is narcissism. What's more, insofar as theater does not arise *ex nihilo* from some societal vacuum, society itself is narcissism. But also, insofar as it feeds and feeds upon one's intellectual *amour propre*, philosophy is narcissism. Rousseau makes the case crystal clear in the 1752 Preface:

> The taste for philosophy slackens all bonds of esteem and goodwill, which tie men to society, and this is perhaps the most dangerous of all evils that it engenders. The charm of study soon renders all other attachment insipid. Moreover, by thinking about humanity, by observing men, the Philosopher learns to appreciate them according to their own worth, *&* it is difficult to really have affection for that which one despises. Soon he reunites in his person all the interest that virtuous men share with their peers: His contempt for others turns to the profit of his pride;

his self-love increases in the same proportion as his indifference to the rest of the universe. The family, the fatherland, become for him empty words without meaning: He is neither parent, nor citizen, nor man; he is a Philosopher.[10]

To return to the question of what brings classics to the stage, our conviction was that if narcissism, pride, and the desire for distinction were powerful features of life in the Eighteenth Century, then this is all the more true at the beginning of the terrified Twenty-First Century, in a world that has become a vast and spectacular hall of mirrors where the only reality is that offered by Reality TV. Unhindered by any egalitarian political vision, our great metropolitan cities have become cathedrals for the celebration of inequality.

10. Rousseau, *Œuvres complètes*, Tome 2, 967. See pp. XII–XIII of this edition.

ACKNOWLEDGMENTS

I have a short list of some important people to thank. I could not have done this translation without you.

Carole Viers-Andronico, for effectively arranging my first full-length literary translation job.

Shawn Robin & Justin Ching, for your willingness to read and comment on the first draft of my manuscript.

Cheyenne Huber, for moling about the mountains of books in Berkeley's library. Your help with researching Montaigne in translation gave me the perfect frame of reference.

Daniel Hugh-Jones, for your careful attention to my final draft, your meticulous proofreader's eye, & most of all, your impeccable ear for language.

COLOPHON

NARCISSUS

was typeset in InDesign CC.

The text & page numbers are set in *Adobe Jenson Pro*.
The titles are set in *Adobe Nyx*.

Book design & typesetting: Alessandro Segalini
Cover design: Contra Mundum Press
Image: Gyula Benczúr, *Narcissus* (1881)

NARCISSUS

is published by Contra Mundum Press.
Its printer has received Chain of Custody certification from:
The Forest Stewardship Council,
The Programme for the Endorsement of Forest Certification,
& The Sustainable Forestry Initiative.

Contra Mundum Press   New York · London · Melbourne

CONTRA MUNDUM PRESS

Dedicated to the value & the indispensable importance of the individual voice, to works that test the boundaries of thought & experience.

The primary aim of Contra Mundum is to publish translations of writers who in their use of form and style are *à rebours*, or who deviate significantly from more programmatic & spurious forms of experimentation. Such writing attests to the volatile nature of modernism. Our preference is for works that have not yet been translated into English, are out of print, or are poorly translated, for writers whose thinking & æsthetics are in opposition to timely or mainstream currents of thought, value systems, or moralities. We also reprint obscure and out-of-print works we consider significant but which have been forgotten, neglected, or overshadowed.

There are many works of fundamental significance to *Weltliteratur* (& *Weltkultur*) that still remain in relative oblivion, works that alter and disrupt standard circuits of thought — these warrant being encountered by the world at large. It is our aim to render them more visible.

For the complete list of forthcoming publications, please visit our website. To be added to our mailing list, send your name and email address to: info@contramundum.net

Contra Mundum Press
P.O. Box 1326
New York, NY 10276
USA

OTHER CONTRA MUNDUM PRESS TITLES

Gilgamesh
Ghérasim Luca, *Self-Shadowing Prey*
Rainer J. Hanshe, *The Abdication*
Walter Jackson Bate, *Negative Capability*
Miklós Szentkuthy, *Marginalia on Casanova*
Fernando Pessoa, *Philosophical Essays*
Elio Petri, *Writings on Cinema & Life*
Friedrich Nietzsche, *The Greek Music Drama*
Richard Foreman, *Plays with Films*
Louis-Auguste Blanqui, *Eternity by the Stars*
Miklós Szentkuthy, *Towards the One & Only Metaphor*
Josef Winkler, *When the Time Comes*
William Wordsworth, *Fragments*
Josef Winkler, *Natura Morta*
Fernando Pessoa, *The Transformation Book*
Emilio Villa, *The Selected Poetry of Emilio Villa*
Robert Kelly, *A Voice Full of Cities*
Pier Paolo Pasolini, *The Divine Mimesis*
Miklós Szentkuthy, *Prae, Vol. 1*
Federico Fellini, *Making a Film*
Robert Musil, *Thought Flights*
Sándor Tar, *Our Street*
Lorand Gaspar, *Earth Absolute*
Josef Winkler, *The Graveyard of Bitter Oranges*
Ferit Edgü, *Noone*

SOME FORTHCOMING TITLES

Jean-Luc Godard, *Phrases*
Pierre Senges, *The Major Refutation*
Claude Mouchard, *Entangled, Papers!, Notes*

www.ingramcontent.com/pod-product-compliance
Lightning Source LLC
Chambersburg PA
CBHW051737090426
42738CB00010B/2303